ADAM WEISHAUPT

A

HUMAN DEVIL

By
Gerald B. Winrod
Editor of The Defender

DEFENDER PUBLISHERS
Wichita, Kansas

ISBN: 978-2-925369-81-3
Printed in the USA.

"The world is governed by very different person-ages from what is imagined by those who are not be-hind the scenes."

——Disraeli

Adam Weishaupt

BEHIND THE SCENES

DISORDERS, revolutions, economic convulsions and political upheavals do not *happen*. They result from planning. Under the surface, unknown to good people, there are constant plots, schemes, tricks and intrigues.

Hidden forces continue their subterranean activities until they reach a boiling point, then an explosion takes place on the surface. The rank and file of people are caught off their guard. There comes a devastating outburst in which lives are lost, property is destroyed, and human development is retarded.

Not until the storm breaks do the sleeping masses awaken, yawn, stir themselves and look about at the wreckage and carnage, after it is too late to help matters. History is replete with examples of this kind.

International conspirators always find it to their advantage to lull the people to sleep until they can get their plots developed so far that nothing can stop them. A man in a stupor is harmless. The despoilers have a way of keeping the popular mind befuddled and drugged, under the influence of their opiates. It is a rare thing for an awakening to take place in time to avert a crisis.

Propaganda is a powerful weapon in the hands of wicked men. Yet the thinking of a whole nation may become warped in a comparatively short time, on some particular question, by a bombardment of ideas released from carefully planned and timed sources. By degrees these ideas sink into the mass mind and a community is moulded accordingly. Then the people take the things they have been taught for granted, little suspecting that, parrot-like, they are merely chattering about false notions which have been insinuated into their mental processes.

Thus designing leaders find it possible to bring wreck and ruin upon a country by pulling wires from behind the scenes. They are able to produce cross currents and create class hatreds, keeping themselves and their true purposes concealed from the public gaze.

The average person lives on the surface and neither cares, nor knows how, to inform himself about hidden evils which may be lurking in the shadows. He prefers to "eat, drink and be merry today", and think no more about the future than absolutely necessary. Try to tell him the unpleasant truth and warn him of what is about to take place, and he is liable to do what the farmer did when he saw a giraffe for the first time, cry out angrily, "I don't believe it!"

The American people are too gullible. They need a new baptism of that good old fashioned virtue called suspicion. The question that haunts me day and night is whether or not it will be possible to awaken them to the impending danger which is close upon us, before it is too late!

Secret societies, sometimes founded upon high ideals and lofty precepts, are frequently prostituted by men of evil genius who get control of them for their own private gain and selfish use. Because there is always an element of mystery associated with a lodge, it becomes a convenient cloak and an ideal means for secret operations, when taken over by subversive influences.

It will be shown in this treatise that certain conspirators have used secret societies in the past as practical vehicles for boring under the surface. Thus, destructive causes, set in motion long ago, are still producing catastrophic effects in the world.

Two revolutions of comparatively recent times,

loom up in the thinking of every student of history. The French revolution and the Russian revolution. Neither of these outbreaks was produced primarily for economic and political reasons in order to relieve the suffering of the poor and middle classes of people. Peaceful means could have been found for adjusting whatever abnormal conditions there may have been existing at the respective periods in which these two storms occurred. It was not necessary to spill an ocean of blood. The fact is that both of these revolutions resulted from secret, under-cover planning so that a certain system, an invisible empire, a hidden organization, could advance its evil interests. The fundamental purpose was to produce an onslaught against Christianity and the moral and social systems which it had produced on the earth.

On July 14, 1856 Disraeli delivered a significant address before England's House of Commons, in which he said, "It is useless to deny, because it is impossible to conceal, that a great part of Europe—the whole of Italy and France and a great portion of Germany, to say nothing of other countries—is covered with a network of these secret societies, just as the superficies of the earth is now being covered with railroads. And what are their objects? They do not attempt to conceal them. They do not want constitutional government; they do not want ameliorated institutions. They want to change the tenure of land, to drive out the present owners of the soil and to put an end to ecclesiastical establishments."

●

ILLUMINISM

THE history of world revolution is bound up in the history of a philosophy—or rather, a disease—known as Illuminism.

The believer in Bible truth discovers in this weird system of occultism a demonic principle capable of warping and twisting the minds of those who allow themselves to come under its influence. The Satanic germ out of which Illuminism unfolds is found in the letter of the Apostle Paul to the Ephesians, "For we wrestle not against flesh and blood, but against principalities, against powers, against the rulers of the darkness of this world, against spiritual wickedness in high places."

As there is a divine illumination which comes into the soul of man through the revealed presence of the Holy Spirit, so also there is a counterfeit light which poisons, blights, blasts, destroys and produces moral decay. There are psychic laws, black mental currents, which, if contacted, will bring one under the conscious control of Satan. There are "seducing spirits" capable of impregnating the human mind with the "doctrines of devils".

There is a white light of spiritual illumination. And there is a black light of Satanic illumination. "Satan himself is transformed into an angel of light." Illuminism is rooted in black magic. It produced a mighty wave of occultism in the eighteenth century which even swept governments from their foundations. And the end is not yet!

These same hidden forces, often using influential leaders as their pawns, are still actively engaged in pushing their program of world chaos with the final objective in view of pulling down the temple of civilization and blotting Christianity from the face of the earth. No matter where we find Illuminism or how we trace its ramifications, Satan is always the Master Mind behind it. Said the Christ, "I beheld Satan as *lightning* fall from heaven." It is true that Satanic light fills the earth; this accounts for the fact that the world is in darkness.

The occult forces from which Illuminism proceeds are as old as the Kingdom of Satan on earth, but for the present we shall trace its rise as a visible organization from the latter part of the fifteenth century. That it goes back to Nimrod and his Babel builders is evident. That it will produce the last great World Dictator, known to students of Bible prophecy as the Antichrist, is probable.

Pausing to consult the Encyclopaedia Britannica, we discover that the term Illuminism has been used for centuries by mystic groups to indicate that "light" had been "directly communicated to them from a higher source, or as due to a clarified and exalted condition of the human intelligence".

The same authority finds Illuminism first emerging from among the Gnostics, which of course takes it back to the beginning of the Christian era. Gnosticism was a filthy, abominable system, invented by the Devil, to pollute and besmirch the early Church in every conceivable manner. It was based upon the twin evils of Spiritualism and immoral sexual practices. It taught the idea that reason surpasses faith.

One of the earliest and most prominent Gnostic leaders was a Jew by the name of Simon Magus. Turning to the volume *Moravians Compared and Detected* by Lavington, we read, "These are heretics, and that they were heretics of the worst kind that ever defiled and disgraced the Christian name, is allowed by all denominations of Christians. Some of these lived in the first century and even in the Apostles' days, but the second century was most fruitful in the production of this generation of vipers.

"Such was the excellency of their knowledge and Illumination, who arrogantly styled themselves Gnostics, that they claimed to be superior to Peter or Paul or any of Christ's other disciples. They only, have drunk up the supreme knowledge, are above principalities and powers, secure of salvation; and for that very reason are free to debauch women, or indulge in all manner of licentiousness. Simon Magus, who taught that his harlot was the Holy Ghost, instituted certain foul and infamous mysteries inexpressibly filthy and had assemblies equally filthy to celebrate them.

"For this end they taught incontinence to be obligatory, as a law; not only lawful, but necessary to salvation; not only compatible with the Savior's religion, but an essential part of it; and those were the best men, who in the common opinion were the most vicious. For which reason, in their feasts, the candles were extinguished, each lay with the women, as chance appointed; and they called this lasciviousness a mystical imitation, a mystical communion. What was abominable in others, being highly meritorious in themselves."

The Gnostic leaders were spiritualist mediums who were reckoned to be in constant communication with "spirits" and from this source came the superior wisdom which this depraved cult was supposed to possess. In the foregoing outline we see the first gleams of that system of Satanic illumination which was to cast its light upon the path of the future.

Historians find the term Illuminism appearing prominently in Spain during the year 1492. It was regarded as being a mixture of occult ideas transplanted from Italy. In the year 1527 Ignatius Loyola, founder of the Jesuits, was arrested by Spanish authorities because of his activities in Illuminati circles.

In Sweden we discover a similar organization putting in its appearance in the early part of the eighteenth century under the name *The Rite of Swedenborg or Illuminati of Stockholm*. The founder of this sect was a spiritualist by the name of Emmanuel Swedenborg. Established in 1721, the Rite has since reached into many parts of the world and is reported to have a considerable following in the United States at the present time. It is another stem from the old root of Gnostic spiritualism.

Wherever the theories of Illuminism are expressed, its exponents invariably profess a superior knowledge over the laws of nature and claim to have all sorts of fantastic powers for making the natural world give up its secrets. They are pictured as possessing mysterious medicines, strange poisons, certain nostrums, an esoteric knowledge of religion, and an understanding of the principles of alchemy. Back in the fourteenth century, the term Rosicrucianism became a cover name for the whole conglomerate mass of occult ideas which Gnostics, Illuminates and their ilk had disseminated during the intervening centuries since Christ. Today, for instance, it is reported that Einstein, the Jew who was expelled from Germany, is a high up Rosicrucian and has been able to communicate with the "Invisible Masters" by means of spiritualism, from which source he is said to have come into possession of his theory of relativity.

Like an interlocking directorate in a business organization, an examination shows that the many demonic lines of occult thought frequently blend, flow together and converge at certain points along the way. From earliest times the dominating factor in the mixture has been the Jewish Cabala.

We are asked to believe that a man by the name of Christian Rosenkrentz was born in Germany in the year 1378. As a young man he made a pilgrimage to the Holy Land. Later he met "Wise Men of Arabia" who helped school him in mystic lore. Then he went to Egypt where he made advanced studies into the mysteries of life, nature and the universe. He plumbed the depths of the Cabala.

Being destined to live 106 years, he died back home

in Europe in 1484. Bringing all the wisdom of the ages together into the one great philosophy which he had created, he revealed his secret to three disciples. He spent the closing days of his life in solitude. His burial place remained a mystery for six times twenty years. In the year 1604 a group of Illuminated ones were guided to his cave. On entering, they were surprised to find it resplendent with a bright light. It contained an altar with a copper plate bearing this inscription, "Living, I reserved this light for my grave."

Mrs. Nesta Webster says, "I suggest that Christian Rosenkrentz was a purely mythical personage, and that the whole legend concerning his travels was invented to disguise the real sources whence the Rosicrucians derived their system, which would appear to have been a compound of ancient esoteric doctrines, of Arabian and Syrian magic, and of Jewish Cabalism. Rosicrucianism thus became in the seventeenth century a generic title by which everything of the nature of Cabalism, Theosophy, Alchemy, Astrology, and Mysticism was designated."

The Rosicrucians pretended to know all sciences, chiefly medicine. They claimed to be masters in strange, mysterious and secret matters; superior in wisdom to the ancient Egyptians, Chaldeans, the Magi or the Apostles.

Four kinds of demons govern the planet, according to Rosicrucian speculators: Earth spirits, Water spirits, Fire spirits and Air spirits.

Enough has now been written to show, in a general way, the true occult character of Illuminism, like an onrushing torrent, pouring through the centuries as a system of black magic which has always existed for the purpose of counterfeiting the pure white truth of the Gospel. With these facts in mind we are ready to come to the subject of our discussion, Adam Weishaupt, who was a man of sufficient capacity to be able to tap in upon this stream of Satanic energy and centralize it into a program of world conquest which he named The Illuminati.

●

ADAM WEISHAUPT

THIS man was born in southern Germany, February 6, 1748. As a comparatively young man we find him occupying the chair of Canon Law in Ingolstadt University. Hidden behind carefully arranged camouflage, he no doubt possessed more power than any other single individual of his day. Through his ability to mould human beings and bend them to his will, he was able to set forces in motion which have since wrecked whole nations and destroyed millions of lives. The impact of his evil genius is still being felt the world around, even down to the present hour.

The plot has been carried on with such secrecy and diabolical cunning that the man's name is scarcely known beyond the circles of research where it has been dug out by students who have a special interest in occult matters and the study of subversive influences. It is, of course, to the advantage of those who are today unloading Weishaupt's schemes upon the world to keep his name and his principles away from the public view. It is remarkable how his followers have succeeded in keeping him out of sight.

Weishaupt used men to carry out his ideas like a carpenter uses tools. Being cognizant of the fact that he was building for the future, that he was moulding generations unborn, he seemed to have no personal vanity that required immediate gratification. He was content to plant the seeds of destruction and allow them plenty of time to germinate. A brilliant writer on subversive movements has said, "It is an unvarying rule of secret societies that the real authors never show themselves."

The French Socialist Freethinker Louis Blanc of the nineteenth century eulogizes Weishaupt as being, "One of the profoundest conspirators who has ever existed." On the other hand, we find Mackey, an American Mason describing him as follows in the book, *Lexicon of Freemasonry*, "Weishaupt was a radical in politics and an infidel in religion, and he organized this association, not more for the purpose of aggrandizing himself, than of overturning Christianity and the institutions of society."

It is pleasant to discover a Mason thus condemning this monster of iniquity because other Masons, particularly in England, have praised him simply because he was able, in his day, to gain control of European Masonry, bend it to his will and use it as an instrument for carrying out his conspiracy against God, Christ, the Church and civilization.

Perhaps this is the time and place to say in capital letters that FREEMASONRY IN AMERICA AND FREEMASONRY IN EUROPE ARE AS DIFFERENT AS DAY IS DIFFERENT FROM NIGHT. This fact should be borne in mind as we proceed to discover how Weishaupt succeeded in perverting the Order in continental Europe, thus using its lodges as underground breeding places of crime, anarchy, atheism and violence.

Parallel attitudes toward Christianity have been discovered in Weishaupt, Voltaire and Frederick the Great. Each gave lip service to the cause of Christ when they found it convenient or expedient to do so, but never failed to improve an opportunity to contribute to its destruction.

Weishaupt took personal credit for the vicious agencies which he started functioning. Hear him as he exlaims, "What it costs me to read, study, think, write, cross out, and re-write!" The dream that was uppermost in his mind was the constant thought of destroying the existing order of society. Being obsessed with this ambition, he looked about for weapons whereby the task could be performed in the shortest possible time. He soon saw what might be accomplished if he could bring the lodge rooms of Europe under his control.

Abbe Barruel, a French patriot and Catholic priest who lived contemporaneously with Weishaupt, wrote freely about the relation of the illumined lodges to the French Revolution. Barruel also made a penetrating examination into the life and personal affairs of the subject of our discussion. "The man who invented his Illuminism only to convert it into the common sewer of every anti-Christian and anti-social error", is the way he speaks of Weishaupt.

In his book *Anti-Christian Conspiracy*, Barruel publishes this interesting statement about a young man who started out to become an Illuminatus but reversed his attitude before he had gone far. The report shows how Weishaupt and his "adepts" always began by giving the prospective initiate small doses, to be increased as the poison started taking effect. "I shall mention Toussaint, as this man shows to what height atheism raged among the conspirators. He had undertaken the part of the corruption of morals. Under the mask of moderation, he succeeds by telling youth that nothing was to be feared from love, this passion only perfecting them. That between man and woman that was a sufficient claim on each other without matrimony. That children are not more beholden to their fathers for their birth than for the champaign they had drunk or the minuet they had been pleased to dance. That vengeance being incompatible with God, the wicked had nothing to fear from the punishments of another world. Notwithstanding all this doctrine the conspirators looked on him as a timid adept because he owned a God in heaven, and a soul in man; and to punish him they styled him the Capuchin Philosopher. Happily for him he took a better way of punishing them by abandoning their cause and recanting from his errors."

To Barruel we are also indebted for information about a man, evidently a Jew, by the name of Kolmer who crossed Weishaupt's trail at the time when his Illuminism was yet in a plastic, formative state. Kolmer, a genius in matters pertaining to black art was, from all indications, a Cabalistic Jew from Egypt. Hearing of Weishaupt, a personal meeting was arranged. The result was, the Satanic impulses which already existed, were deepened in the soul of the man who was destined to wield a lasting influence for evil upon the lives of countless millions.

Five years intervened between the time that Kolmer called on Weishaupt and the day when the latter officially announced that he was ready to accept members into his new order. In other words, several years were spent in careful planning, thinking out methods, and making deliberate preparations to attack God and the governments of the world.

At last Weishaupt was ready to announce, "That we shall have a Masonic lodge of our own. That we shall regard this as our nursery garden. That to some of these Masons we shall not at once reveal that we have something more than the Masons have. That at every opportunity we shall cover ourselves with this (Masonry). All those who are not suited to the work shall remain in the Masonic Lodge and advance in that without knowing anything of the further system."

Thus, he succeeded in creating a super-Masonry with himself in the position of dominant power. He produced something which he led Masons to believe was of a higher character, much older and more mysterious than anything they had. Before a great while he was able to put his key men into all the strategic positions of Masonry which made it possible for him to sit back and pull wires from within the shadows.

More will be said about this later, but let it be remembered that in everything Weishaupt said and did, he was always animated with just one desire, namely to destroy, destroy, destroy! When he ruled Masonry, he did it with this one thought in mind— to use it as an instrument of destruction so as to accomplish his secret aims, the extermination of Christianity and the leveling of all governments to the ground.

In his personal life, this man was a moral pervert. He lived in incestuous relationship with his sister-in-law. When it was discovered that she was to give birth to a child he became seized with fear and planned an abortion. From documents which fell into the hands of the German government it has been discovered that his organization possessed dreadful poisons and had no hesitation about using them when to do so might serve to silence an enemy or advance their cause in other ways.

They had a powder which produced blindness, a prescription of a poison which had an insidiously slow but deadly effect, the formula for another poison which "devoured everything" when sprayed into the face, etc. They also possessed a strange substance called *Luisenwasser* (Louise Water) because it was secretly given to Louise, the Crown Princess of Saxony to further the romance with Toselli and thereby detract from the reputation of the ruling dynasty. These secrets were all made known to the Bavarian government when it confiscated the lodge property of the organization on August 16, 1785.

In their collection of poisons and weird chemical

comprods they had abortive remedies and it was
to these that Weishaupt resorted in his fright when he
learned of the physical condition of his sister-in-law.
He wished to make a suitable abortive, the formula
of which was known to the organization. He wrote
a distracted letter to a doctor who was a fellow member, "We have already tried several things to get rid
of the child. She herself is willing to undertake everything. But Euriphon is too timid."

Fate later delivered this letter into the hands of
government officials with a key to the code in which
it was written whereby it was made understandable
to the authorities. It contained a further reference to
"Celsus" who "could certainly help me and had already
promised to do so three years ago, etc." The last
sentence shows that this monster of vice had been
occupying himself with abortive remedies already for
three years.

The abortion failed and the child, a male, was born
January 30, 1784.

●

THE ILLUMINATI

TWO mighty avenues of thought, one occult and the
other militaristic, converged upon the diseased
brain of this wicked personage. The first was the
Illuminism of centuries past and the second was the
Jesuit order which was founded in the year 1541.

It has been shown above that the roots of the
system known as Illuminism reach far back into Gnosticism. The momentum of demonism continued to
increase until it became a mighty tidal wave in
the latter half of the eighteenth century. Weishaupt was caught on its crest and proved equal
to the task of capturing and imprisoning the force of

the movement within the four walls of the new organization which he was then building. From the angle of the occult, it is clearly seen that the doctrines of Weishaupt were not new. His genius was rather in the fact that he was able to compress the demonic principles, with which he was dealing, into a system.

While other systems of Illuminism had previously existed, Weishaupt's became *the* Illuminati. It is well attested that his Order assumed fundamentally the right of life and death. To his group it meant nothing to snuff out a life if in so doing their sinister aims were advanced. Hence the use of strange poisons and weird medicines. The use of chemicals and such things shows an unmistakable link between the Illuminati and Rosicrucianism, both of which had a common origin.

While Barruel, a Catholic, was assembling his material about the plot in France, another scholar by the name of John Robison, a Scotch Protestant, was carrying on a similar investigation in the British Isles. Robison's book was published under the imposing title *"Proofs of a Conspiracy against all the Religions and Governments of Europe, carried on by secret meetings of Free Masons, Illuminati and Reading Societies, collected from good authorities by the Author, Professor of Natural Philosophy and Secretary of the Royal Society of Edinburgh."* The work was published in 1798.

After examining the writings of Barruel, Robison wrote, "This author (Barruel) confirms all that I have said of the Enlighteners, whom he very aptly calls Philosophists; and of the abuses of Freemasonry in France. He shows, unquestionably, that a formal and systematic conspiracy against Religion was formed and zealously prosecuted by Voltaire, d'Alembert and Diderot, assisted by Frederick II, King of Prussia; and I see that their principles and their manner of procedure have been the same with those of the German atheists and anarchists.

"Like them they hired an army of writers; they industriously pushed their writings into every house and every cottage. Those writing were equally calculated for inflaming the sensual appetites of men and for perverting their judgments. They endeavored to get the command of the schools, particularly those for the lower classes; and they erected and managed a prodigious number of Circulating Libraries and Reading Societies. They took the name of Economists and affected to be continually occupied with plans for improving Commerce, Manufactures, Agriculture, Finance, etc., and published from time to time respectable performances on those subjects.

"But their darling project was to destroy Christianity and all Religion, and to bring about a total change of government. They employed writers to compose corrupting and impious books—these were revised by the Society and corrected until they suited their purpose. A number were printed in a handsome manner, to defray the expense; and then a greater number were printed in the cheapest form possible and given for nothing, or at very low prices to hawkers and peddlers with the injunction to distribute them secretly through the cities and villages."

If Professor Robison was living today he could not describe more accurately the tricks and schemes which are being employed before our eyes for the accomplishment of the same objective that the Illuminati had in mind. Some people think Communism is only a blood and thunder proposition sponsored by men who are capable of throwing brickbats and bombs. This is far from the truth. The more dangerous conspirator is the one who occupies a chair in a class-room and insinuates his poison into centers of learning. The connection between the Illuminati and modern Communism will be shown presently as being self evident.

While the Illuminati possessed an esoteric mystical side that appealed to lodge members, yet this was not the phase in which Weishaupt was most deeply concerned. All of this mysterious glamour was, to him, only a means toward an end. Mrs. Webster remarks significantly, "On the contrary, the more we penetrate into his system, the more apparent it becomes that all the formulas he employs which derive from any religious source—whether Persian, Egyptian, or Christian—merely serve to distinguish a purely material purpose, a plan for destroying the existing order of society."

Mrs. Webster is right. Weishaupt's chief aim in life was world revolution. He simply prostituted Masonry because he found it to be the most practical tool available for the accomplishment of his devilish purposes. To beguile Masons and capture the Order he worked out an elaborate system of secret degrees through which his followers were led step by step and finally graduated in his "mysteries".

Men who came under his hypnotic spell soon found their minds so confused that they were no longer capable of looking at life through normal eyes. Local lodges, thus polluted, became spawns for breeding vice and revolution. It was in these underground centers that the revolutionary activity which produced the French Revolution was hatched out. Masonic units, dotted by the thousands all over the map of Europe, were thus transformed into places of anarchy, devoted to creating mob violence.

An *Illuminized lodge* was one that had become thoroughly trained in the principles of Weishaupt and the technique of revolution. By this means he was able to bore beneath the surface and undermine every government in Europe.

For the sake of thoroughness we will pause to outline the various degrees which constituted the path of advancement in Illuminized Masonry. These degrees were evolved by Weishaupt personally.

(The first Class)

First Degree. Minerval degree or Preparatory Seminary.

Second Degree. The Lesser Illuminate or Illuminatus Minor.

(Special note: These two degrees were divided into five.)

1. The Preparatory.
2. The Novitiate.
3. The Minerval degree (from Minerval).
4. The Little first degree.
5. The Great first degree.

(The second Class)

Third Degree. The three degrees of the Masonry of St. John:

Apprentice.
Journeyman.
Master.

Fourth Degree. The greater Illuminate (Illuminatus Major).

The Scotch Novitiate.

Fifth Degree. The directing Illuminate (Illuminatus Dirigens).

The Scotch Knights.

(The third Class)

A. The Small Mysteries:
Sixth Degree. Priest's Degree.
Seventh Degree. Regent's Degree.
B. The Great Mysteries:
Eighth Degree. Magus.
Ninth Degree. Rex.

Degrees eight and nine were not even supposed to have existed.

It can not be emphasized too strongly that Weishaupt's true purpose was not to advance the cause of Masonry. In reality he despised the Order. His consuming ambition was simply to use it as a means toward an end. Professor Robison's careful analysis shows that Weishaupt's program of destruction embodies the six following fundamental propositions:

1. Abolition of all ordered government.
2. Abolition of inheritance.
3. Abolition of private property.
4. Abolition of patriotism.
5. Abolition of family.
6. Abolition of religion.

The foregoing arrangement, when carried out, means but one thing—THE BREAK DOWN OF THE WORLD.

These are the six basic principles of Communism as we know it today. Each of these have been applied in Russia. The modern "Weishaupts" of Moscow expect to carry his dream through to completion and wreck the entire world before they finish. A little deep thinking will show that Communism is not a new thing; in these studies we are taking the Red menace back to May 1, 1776, the day the Illuminati was officially brought into existence.

●

THE JESUITS

WEISHAUPT was trained as a Jesuit. He later renounced the organization. He may or may not have been sincere in his change of attitude but the fact remains that the fierceness of this Roman Catholic militaristic Order fastened its influence upon him. It left an impression that contributed to all of his future inventions and decisions. A short detour into the nature and purposes of this organization will give an insight into the forces which helped to mould the character of the man.

The story of the Society of Jesus (Jesuits) is interesting, but far from inspiring. It is the "army" of the Roman Church and has behind it a trail of Protestant blood which it will never be able to wash away. It is a vast, powerful, world-wide machine with a reputation for moving swift and terrible! A modern writer calls them the Black International.

Credit is given for the founding of the Order to Ignatius Loyola on April 5, 1541. It will be recalled the Loyola was previously arrested by the Spanish government for subversive activities as a Gnostic. He was not convicted. Disraeli, the Jewish Premier of England, said in his book *Coningsby*, "You never observe a great intellectual movement in Europe in which the Jews do not greatly participate. The first Jesuits were Jews."

The Jesuits make their headquarters in the Vatican at Rome. The head of the Order is known as the General. His position is that of Commander-in-chief and he wields absolute power over the members who are pledged to blind obedience. The General claims his authority from the Pope. Each member makes a series of vows and takes certain secret oaths. The "fourth vow" is known to be one of special allegiance to the Pope, promising to go in obedience to him whensoever and whithersoever he may demand. Jesuits have been dubbed "the secret service men of the Vatican".

Because the General of the Jesuits always wears a black garb he is familiarly known as the "Black Pope".

There have been times when Popes have refused

to countenance Jesuitical crimes and have curtailed or disbanded the Order. An instance of this kind occurred on July 21, 1773 when the Pope abolished them at the demand of the governments of France, Spain, Portugal, Naples and Austria. But they were soon back in the fold stronger than ever. Today they are reported to be active in all parts of the world.

In her treatise *Occult Theocracy* Lady Queenborough takes the following quotation from a manuscript entitled *Histoire des Congregations et Sodalites Jesuitiques Depuis 1563 jusqu' au temps present*, which she found in Rue Richelieu library at Paris:

"Initiation. — From this, as well as other works, we gather some of the ceremonies with which aspirants were initiated into the Order. Having in nearly all Roman Catholic countries succeeded in becoming the educators of the young, they were able to mould the youthful mind according to their secret aims. If then, after a number of years, they detected in the pupil a blind and fanatic faith, conjoined with exalted pietism and indomitable courage, they proceeded to initiate him; in the opposite case, they excluded him. The proofs lasted twenty-four hours, for which the candidate was prepared by long and severe fasting, which, by prostrating his bodily strength, inflamed his fancy, and, just before the trial, a powerful drink was administered to him. Then the mystic scene began—diabolical apparitions, evocation of the dead, representations of the flames of hell, skeletons, moving skulls, artificial thunder and lightning, in fact, the whole paraphernalia and apparatus of the ancient mysteries. If the neophyte, who was closely watched, showed fear or terror, he remained for ever in the inferior degree; but if he bore the proof well, he was advanced to a higher grade.

"At the initiation into the second degree (Scholastici) the same proofs, but on a grander scale, had to be undergone. The candidate, again prepared for them by long fastings, was led with his eyes bandaged into a large cavern, resounding with wild howlings and roarings which he had to traverse, reciting at the same time prayers specially appointed for that occasion. At the end of the cave he had to crawl through a narrow opening, and while doing this, the bandage was taken from his eyes by an unseen hand, and he found himself in a square dungeon, whose floor was covered with a mortuary cloth, on which stood three lamps, shedding a feeble light on the skulls and skeletons ranged around. This was the Cave of Evocation, the Black Chamber, so famous in the annals of the Fathers. Here, giving himself up to prayer, the neophyte passed some time, during which the priests could, without his being aware of it, watch his every movement and gesture. If his behavior was satisfactory, all at once two brethren, representing archangels, presented themselves before him, without his being able to tell whence they had so suddenly started up,— a good deal can be done with properly fitted and oiled trap-doors,—and, observing perfect silence, bound his forehead with a white band soaked with blood, and covered with hieroglyphics; they then hung a small crucifix round his neck, and a small satchel containing relics, or what did duty for them. Finally, they took off all his clothing, which they cast on a pyre in one corner of the cave, and marked his body with numerous crosses, drawn with blood. At this point, the hierophant with his assistants entered, and, having bound a red cloth round the middle of the candidate's body, the brethren, clothed in bloodstained garments, placed themselves beside him, and drawing their daggers, formed the steel arch over his head. A carpet being then spread on the floor, all knelt down and prayed for about an hour, after which the pyre was secretly set on fire; the further wall of the cave opened, the air resounded with strains, now gay, now lugubrious, and a long procession of spectres, phantoms, angels, and demons filed past the neophyte like the 'supers' in a pantomime. Whilst this farce was going on, the candidate took the following oath:—'In the name of Christ crucified, I swear to burst the bonds that yet unite me to father, mother, brothers, sisters, relations, friends; to the King, magistrates, and any other authority, to which I may ever have sworn fealty, obedience, gratitude, or service. I renounce . . . . the place of my birth, henceforth to exist in another sphere. I swear to reveal to my new superior, whom I desire to know, what I have done, thought, read, learnt, or discovered, and to observe and watch all that comes under my notice. I swear to yield myself up to my superior, as if I were a corpse, deprived of life and will. I finally swear to flee temptation, and to reveal all I succeed in discovering, well aware that lightning is not more rapid and ready than the dagger to reach me wherever I may be.'

"The new member having taken this oath, was then introduced into a neighboring cell, where he took a bath, and was clothed in garments of new and white linen. He finally repaired with the other brethren to a banquet, where he could with choice food and wine compensate himself for his long abstinence, and the horrors and fatigues he had passed through."

Events in the history of the Jesuits seem to bear out the supposition that both Jews and Catholics have at times united their efforts in its ranks to bring about destruction of Protestantism. To illustrate, during the years 1573 to 1580, the international General was a Belgian Jew by the name of Eberhard Mercurian. Thus we see a Jew Jesuit and a Gentile Pope working together (a "mutual adulation society") in a frantic effort to put Protestantism on the gallows. The present General is a Pole by nationality, his name being Vladimir Ledochowski.

The real reason for establishing the Society of Jesus was to check the progress of the Reformation which broke upon the world in the little town of Wittenberg, Germany, October 31, 1517. While the Jesuits failed in their attempt to blot Protestantism out of existence, yet they did succeed in stopping the growth of the movement in southern Germany and other countries of Europe.

No one has taken the trouble to deny that the Order exists down to the present time for the same purpose —namely a flank attack upon Protestants and their faith. The leading principle of the Jesuits sounds good enough, love of God and of their fellow men, but into their constitution there was written another principle, "the end justifies the means". In other words, when occasion demands it, any moral law may be transgressed to promote the interests of the Church. Someone has called this arrangement "Holy hellishness".

Many vicious crimes have been laid at the door of the Jesuits in the past, notably the Gun Powder Plot in England, and the killing of the Huguenots in France.

I recall while being shown through the Parliament buildings in London, we paused at a certain place and was told that if the Gun Powder Plot had been carried out in 1605, as planned by the Jesuits, the King and members of Parliament would have been destroyed. Thirty-six barrels of gun powder, more than a ton, had been stored in the basement ready to be exploded when the sessions of government convened. The plot was not discovered until two days before Parliament met.

The scheme was traced to the Jesuits and some of their leaders in England were put to death as a result.

But the most heinous crime of which the Jesuits have ever been guilty was the slaughtering of the unsuspecting Huguenots on Sunday, August 24, 1572.

It was on the day of St. Bartholomew—a quiet Sunday in Paris. Suddenly the bells of the St. Germain began to ring. I shall never forget the chill that came over me as I walked through the door of this building for the first time, realizing as I did that this was the place where the signal was given to massacre the Protestants.

Like a cat springs upon an unsuspecting bird, so the Jesuits sprang upon the defenseless Protestants. Coligny, the leader of the Huguenots, was among those put to death in this awful orgy of blood. From Paris, the massacre soon spread to other cities, and it has been estimated that no less than one hundred thousand Protestants were wiped out.

Weishaupt may have tried conscientiously to separate himself from the Jesuits but the early influence of the Order lingered with him throughout his life. Even if he did divorce himself from the visible organization, he had already assimilated its intangible principles. That he drew upon the Jesuits for methods and nomenclature is readily admitted by careful students of the man and his work.

Gould, in his *History of Freemasory*, remarks, "He (Weishaupt) had unconsciously imbibed that most pernicious doctrine that the end justifies the means".

FRENCH REVOLUTION

AFTER spending years in investigating the Illuminati and its ramifications, Professor Robison felt prompted to write, "We assert with confidence, that the Mason lodges in France were hot-beds where the seeds were sown, and tenderly reared, of all the pernicious doctrines which soon after choked every moral or religious cultivation, and have made the Society worse than a waste, have made it a noisome marsh of human corruption filled with every rank and poisonous weed. It was in this respect that the Mason lodges contributed to the dissemination of dangerous opinions and they were employed for this purpose all over the Kingdom. And thus it appears that Germany had experienced the same gradual progress, from Religion to Atheism, from decency to dissoluteness, and from loyalty to rebellion, which has had its course in France. Freemasonry is innocent of all these things; but Freemasonry has been abused, and at last totally perverted —and so will and must any such secret organization, as long as men are licentious in their opinions or wicked in their dispositions."

Weishaupt's trickery in directing things from behind the scenes is disclosed in the following letter written by him to a fellow Illuminatus, "We must consider how we can begin to work under another form. If only the aim is achieved, it does not matter under what cover it takes place, and a cover is always necessary. For in concealment lies a great part of our strength. For this reason we must cover ourselves with the name of another society. The lodges that are under Freemasonry are in the meantime the most suitable cloak for our high purpose, because the world is already accustomed to expect nothing great from them which merits attention. As in the spiritual Orders of the Roman Church, religion was, alas! only a pretense, so must our Order also in a nobler way try to conceal itself behind a learned society or something of the kind. A society concealed in this manner cannot be worked against. We shall be shrouded in impenetrable darkness from spies and emissaries of other societies."

The manner in which Masons were frequently misled is illustrated by a letter from a leader by the name of Cato to Weishaupt, "Now that he (a new prospect) is a Mason I have put all about this Illuminati before him, shown him what is unimportant and at this opportunity taken up the general plan of our Illuminati, and as this pleased him I said that such a thing really existed, whereat he gave me his word that he would enter it."

Showing how they sought to capture whole lodges, the following letter was sent by a member named Philo to Weishaupt, "I have now found in Cassel the best man, on whom I cannot congratulate ourselves enough: he is Mauvillion, Grand Master of one of the Royal York Lodges. So with him we have the whole lodge in our hands. He has also got from them all their miserable degrees."

Mounier, a French writer left this record in one of his reports, "Weishaupt made the acquaintance of a Hanoverian, the Baron von Knigge, a famous intriguer, long practised in the charlatanism of lodges of Freemasons. On his advice new degrees were added to the old ones, and it was resolved to profit by Freemasonry whilst profoundly despising it. They decided that the degrees of Entered Apprentice, Fellow Craft, Master Mason, and Scotch Knight should be added to those of the Illuminati, and that they would boast of possessing exclusively the real secrets of the Freemasons and affirm that Illuminism was the real primitive Freemasonry."

Not until the government confiscated the property of the Illuminati was it possible to penetrate its secrets and really get at the man behind the system. On one occasion Weishaupt wrote to an intimate friend, "My circumstances necessitate that I should remain hidden from most of the members as long as I live. I am obliged to do everything through five or six persons." On another occasion he said, "One must show how easy it would be for one clever head to direct hundreds of thousands of men."

Again he wrote, "I have two immediately below me into whom I breathe my whole spirit, and each of these two has again two others, and so on. In this way I can set a thousand men in motion and on fire in the simplest manner, and in this way one must impart orders and operate on politics."

Shortly before the French Revolution, in the latter part of the eighteenth century, we find the Marquis de Luchet saying, "This society aims at governing the world. Its object is universal domination." He called the Illuminati "a subterranean fire smouldering eternally and breaking forth periodically in violent and devastating explosions." He pleaded with Masons, as a whole, to get their eyes open and save their Order from these corrupting influences. "Would it not be possible to direct the Freemasons themselves against the Illumines by showing them that whilst they are working to maintain harmony in society, those others everywhere are sowing seeds of discord?"

In plain language the program of Illuminized Freemasonry was simply a plan for upsetting the whole world by revolutions. When it captured the lodge rooms of Europe, the plan truly became a "subterranean fire." The first great explosion took place in what we know in history as the French Revolution. Imagine thousands of lodge rooms converted into nests of human vipers, men possessing warped intellects with one uncontrollable impulse surging through their arteries—destruction! destruction! destruction!—and you will be getting down to the true cause of the holocaust which drenched the French nation in human blood.

"What was the aim of this occult power?" asks Mrs. Webster. "Was it merely the plan of destruction that had originated in the brain of a Bavarian professor twenty years earlier, or was it something far older, a live and terrible force that had lain dormant through the centuries, that Weishaupt and his allies had not created but only loosed upon the world? The Reign of Terror, like the outbreak of Satanism in the Middle Ages, can be explained by no material causes —the orgy of hatred, lust, and cruelty directed not only against the rich but still more against the poor and defenceless, the destruction of science, art, and beauty, the desecration of the churches, the organized campaign against all that was noble, all that was sacred, all that humanity holds dear, what was this but Satanism?

"'To those who lived through it, it seemed that France lay under the sway of the powers of darkness. So in the 'great shipwreck of civilization', as a contemporary has described it, the projects of the Cabalists, the Gnostics, and the secret societies which for nearly eighteen centuries had sapped the foundations of Christianity found their fulfillment."

It is a fact that the powers of the Devil cause such outbursts as the French Revolution, but it is also true that these powers manifest themselves through human beings. There is no difficulty in discovering who were the obsessed personalities that permitted themselves to become the instruments of Satan in bringing this great sorrow upon the French people.

"We will have no God, no masters," shouted the mobs, not knowing that they were merely croaking like frogs, repeating the ideas inculcated by Weishaupt and his followers. Then they picked up a woman from the streets of Paris, dressed her in costly robes and profaned the Cathedral of Notre Dame by worshipping her as the Goddess of Reason. In prostrating themselves before this new god, the jeering crowds little knew that they were surrendering to the philosophy of the ancient Gnostics who boasted that Reason was superior to Faith.

Weishaupt was hidden so deep in the shadows that

no one suspected his connection with the Goddess in Notre Dame. But long before her appearance, he had introduced the secret poison which was then becoming manifest. He eulogized Reason as the supreme factor in religion. Here were his words, "When at last Reason becomes the religion man, so will the problem be solved."

At another time he wrote, "Freemasonry is hidden Christianity, at least my explanations of the hieroglyphics fit this perfectly; and in the way in which I explain Christianity no one need be ashamed to be a Christian, for I leave the name and substitute for it Reason."

By the method of deduction used above of identifying Reason as an integral part of the Weishaupt code, it is possible to trace every phase of the French Revolution to some part of the Illuminati program behind the scenes. In other words, when lightning struck on the surface of France, it was merely the visible effect of hidden causes which had been carefully planned and timed by the conspirators. The events starting in 1789 were only Illuminism in action. And no informed person will say that the planning has ceased! The same plot is being carried out today through secret and subterranean channels.

There is an abundance of proof that such leaders of the Revolution as Lafayette, Mirabeau, Garat, Marat, Robespierre, Danton, Desmoulins and many others, were active members of Illuminized Masonic lodges. From this source they got their ideas, acquired their fierceness and worked out their plots.

Every student of history will recall that the political clubs known as the Jacobins, held the balance of power throughout the French Revolution. Among the early members of these mysterious organizations were Mirabeau and Robespierre. The Encyclopaedia Britannica says, "By August 10, 1790 there were already one hundred and fifty-two affiliated clubs, and at the close of 1791 the Jacobins had a network of branches all over France. It was this widespread yet highly centralized organization that gave to the Jacobin Club its formidable power. The secret of their strength was this: in the midst of general disorganization, they alone were organized."

From the time the first Jacobin Club was organized, these centers were duly Illuminated by Weishaupt's principal helpers, including Bode and Baron de Busche. The basic purpose of the Jacobins was "to further the triumph of dogmatic Atheism and create a great social upheaval". The French writer Le Forestier explains, "The members charged with spreading the propaganda of the subversive principles of the club numbered fifty thousand. In 1790, it had twenty thousand livres at its disposal, but by the end of 1791, these had increased to thirty millions".

The history of the unspeakable Terror of the French Revolution is the history of the Jacobins. And the history of the Jacobins is the history of the Illuminati. Let it be remembered that one of Weishaupt's affectionate titles was "PATRIARCH OF THE JACOBINS".

After the storm of the Revolution subsided, the power to govern France was vested in the *Comite de Salut Public* composed of three hundred men, all leaders in the Illuminated Masonic Order. Lady Queenborough remarks, "The particular brand of Communism favored by the conspirators was based on the theory that the poor could not help themselves or improve their position, that the rich must be suppressed and that the ideal state could be reached by class war, and a dictatorship of the proletariat."

Even a casual examination of the forces at work in the French Revolution compared with those which swept Russia eighteen years ago, will show a remarkable similarity. It has been aptly remarked that the Russian Revolution began where the French Revolution ended.

Parenthetically, it is interesting to notice that in Germany, all secret orders have been disbanded under the Hitler regime. Everything must be done in the open and in plain sight. No fraternal secrets are permitted. The Masonic Order, the Illuminati and all other such societies have been destroyed.

Mussolini inaugurated the same policy when he first ascended to power in Italy. His *Autobiography*, published in 1928, contains many interesting statements regarding Italian Masonry which may be appropriately repeated here, by virtue of the present discussion:

"The Fascisti, as intelligent people worthy of the epoch in which they were living, followed me in the new conception of religious policy. To it was attached our war against Masonry as we knew Masonry in Italy. It was a war of fundamental importance and Fascism was almost unanimous in a determination to fight it to the end.

"Let us not forget that the Masons of Italy have always represented a distortion, not only in political life, but in spiritual concepts. All the strength of Masonry was directed against the papal policies, but this struggle represented no real and profound ideal. The secret society from a practical point of view rested on an association of mutual adulation, of reciprocal aid, of pernicious nepotism and favoritism. To become powerful and to consummate its underhanded dealings, Masonry made use of the weaknesses of the Liberal governments that succeeded each other in Italy after 1870 to extend its machinations in the bureaucracy, in the magistracy, in the field of education, and also in the army, so that it could dominate the vital ganglions of the whole nation. Its secret character throughout the twentieth century, its mysterious meetings, abhorrent to our beautiful communities with their sunlight and their love of truth, gave to the sect the character of corruption, a crooked concept of life, without programme, without soul, without moral value.

"My antipathy for that disgusting form of secret association goes back to my youth. Long before, at the Socialist congress of Ancona in 1914, I had presented to my comrades the dilemma: Socialists or Masons? That point of view had won a complete triumph, in spite of the strong opposition of the Mason-socialists.

"Later, in Fascism, I made the same gesture of strength. It took courage. I obeyed the positive command of my conscience, and not any opportunism. My attitude had nothing in common with the anti-Masonic spirit of the Jesuits. They acted for reasons of defense. After all, their inner organization as a religious society is almost completely unknown.

"For my direct, methodical and consistent course of policy the hate of the Masonic sect persecutes me even now. Masonry of that type has been beaten in Italy, but it operates and conspires behind the mask of the international anti-Fascism. It utterly fails to defeat me. It tries to throw mud at me, but the insult does not reach its mark. It machinates plots and crimes, but the hired assassins do not control my destiny. It goes gossiping about my weaknesses, and the supposed organic afflictions of my body, but I am more alive and stronger than ever.

"This is a war without quarter, a war of which I am a veteran. Every time that I have wanted to cauterize difficult situations in Italian political life, every time that I have wanted to give a sincere, frank and loyal moral rectitude to the personnel in politics, I have always had against me our Masonry! But that organization, which in other times was very powerful, has been beaten by me. Against me it did not and cannot win. Italians won this battle for me. They found the cure for this leprosy."

But the sequel to the above story is that since Mussolini wrote these words, he has been prevailed upon to restore to Masons their previous liberties. In August 1930 the *Rosicrucian Digest*, published in California, printed the following significant announcement, "The recent decision on the part of Mussolini permitting Freemasons and Rosicrucians of Italy to hold lodge sessions and to conduct their work again under a national council composed of their own members and officers, will result in a rapid revival of work in Italy."

Reports from England declare that powerful Jewish influences close to Mussolini were responsible for his reversal of policy.

Before drawing this part of the discussion to a close, perhaps a final word from Barruel would be proper, in which he laments over the fact that the French people were so stupefied that they could not see the impending Revolution directly in front of them. He says, "To give the fatal impulse to the world, it now only remained for the sect to carry its mysteries into a nation powerful and active indeed, but unfortunately more susceptible of that effervescence which bereaves man of the power of thinking, than of that judgment which foresees disasters; to a nation which, in its ardor and enthusiasm, too easily forgets that true greatness is not that courage which bids defiance to danger (for the vandals and barbarious can boast of such heroes); to a nation, in short, that has ever been a prey to allusions, and which, before it would hearken to the councils of wisdom, might in its fury overturn the altar and shiver the sceptre, returning to reason only in time to weep over the ruins and lament the devastation of which it has been the cause."

JEWISH CONTROL

WHEN good, law abiding Masons in Europe realized what had happened to their order after the French Revolution they became sick at heart and discouraged. Not until it was too late to correct the situation did they come to understand what had happened. This was particularly noticeable in Germany where the Grand Master, the Duke of Brunswick, issued a Manifesto to all the German lodges in 1794 declaring that European Masonry had been completely perverted by the new sect, the Illuminati. In his utter despondency he advocated disbanding the Order entirely.

I shall quote his famous Manifesto in part, "A great sect arose which, taking for its motto the good and the happiness of man, worked in the darkness of the conspiracy to make the happiness of humanity a prey for itself. This sect is known to everyone: its brothers are known no less than its name. It is they who have undermined the foundations of the Order to the point of complete overthrow; it is by them that all humanity has been poisoned and led astray for several generations. The ferment that reigns amongst the peoples is their work. They founded the plans of their insatiable ambition on the political pride of nations. Their founders arranged to introduce this pride into the heads of the peoples. They began by casting odium on religion . . . . They invented the rights of man which it is impossible to discover even in the book of Nature, and they urged the people to wrest from their princes the recognition of these supposed rights. The plan they had formed for breaking all social ties and of destroying all order was revealed in all their speeches and acts. They deluged the world with a multitude of publications; they recruited apprentices of every rank and in every position; they deluded the most perspicacious men by falsely alleging different intentions. They sowed in the hearts of youth the seed of covetousness, and they excited it with the bait of the most insatiable passions. Indomitable pride, thirst of power, such were the only motives of this sect: their masters had nothing less in view than the thrones of the earth, and the government of the nations was to be directed by their nocturnal clubs.

"This is what has been done and is still being done. But we notice that princes and people are unaware how and by what means this is being accomplished. That is why we say to them in all frankness: The misuse of our Order, the misunderstanding of our secret, has produced all the political and moral troubles with which the world is filled today. You who have been initiated, you must join yourselves with us in raising your voices, so as to teach peoples and princes that the sectarians, the apostates of our Order, have alone been and will be the authors of present and future revolutions. We must assure princes and peoples, on our honour and our duty, that our association is in no way guilty of these evils. But in order that our attestations should have force and merit belief, we must make for princes and people a complete sacrifice; so as to cut out to the roots the abuse and error, we must from this moment dissolve the whole Order. This is why we destroy and annihilate it completely for the time; we will preserve the foundations for posterity, which will clear them when humanity, in better times, can derive some benefit from our holy alliance."

Adam Weishaupt lived to the age of eighty-two. He continued his criminal activities against civilization for many years after the French Revolution. *For the sake of emphasis, let it be remarked once more that Masonry in both England and the United States has always been unlike the Masonry of continental Europe which can best be designated by the use of the term Grand Orient.*

The real conspirators behind the Illuminati were Jews. The whole scheme was a Jewish plot to the core. Bernard Lazare, a well known Jewish writer, says, "There were Jews, Cabalistic Jews, around Weishaupt". One must also bear in mind the influence of Kolmer, the mysterious Jew from the east, upon the mind of Weishaupt even prior to the birth of the Illuminati.

Confiscated documents of the organization disclose that of the thirty-nine chief sub-leaders of Weishaupt, seventeen were Jews. Illuminati-Hall of Ingolstadt, where Weishaupt lived, was later transformed into a synagogue.

The Jewish method of exhausting their Gentile environment has always been to stir up strife from secret sources and engender class hatreds. This was the plan used in bringing about the death of Christ; a mob spirit was created. The same policy is described in Acts 14:2, "But the unbelieving Jews *stirred up the Gentiles*, and made their minds evil affected against the brethren."

In indicting his own race, Lazare says, "The complaint of the anti-Semites seems to be founded: the Jew has the revolutionary spirit; consciously or not he is an agent of revolution."

Returning to Mrs. Webster, we are told that the Jew who turns himself over to subversive activities becomes "a formidable hidden power". "Nevertheless, in modern revolutions the part played by the Jews cannot be ignored, and the influence they have exercised will be seen on examination to have been twofold —financial and occult. Throughout the Middle Ages it is as sorcerers and usurers that they incur the reproaches of the Christian world, and it is still the same role, under the more modern terms of magicians and loan-mongers, that we detect their presence behind the scenes of revolution from the seventeenth century onward."

The plan used by the Jewish leaders of the Illuminati to keep informed concerning all Gentile activities and to know what wires to pull so as to produce confusion, was to require every member to spy constantly on his fellow members. So, once a month, each Illuminatus was compelled to hand to his superior officer a sealed envelope containing information about his friends. It bore the title *quibus licet* and was to be conveyed to the unknown ruler at the top of the Order's pyramid. The individual member down the line was kept in the dark, knowing only one leader above him, to whom he had taken the oath of blind obedience. The Gentile dupes were taught to think that they were parts of a great plan, and not concerning themselves to learn that they had allowed themselves to become helpless cogs in a merciless wheel which was created for the purpose of grinding the Gentile nations to powder.

This system has been expanded in our day to cover the entire Russian Empire concerning which it has truthfully been said, "everybody is a spy spying on a spy". Every fundamental principle of the Illuminati may be traced through the French Revolution, down to the present hour through the avenue of international Communism.

One of the closest men to Weishaupt was a Jew by the name of Cagliostro. His real name was Joseph Balsamo but he took the lodge name Comte de Cagliostro. He traveled through Greece and Egypt and knew the occult secrets of the Jewish Cabala. He was on the inner circle of the Illuminati and had much to do with wrecking European Masonry and changing it into an instrument for producing carnage. A close associate of Cagliostro was the Swabian doctor Mesmer whose evil hypnotic science still bears the name of Mesmerism.

Since the Jews have always controled the main arteries or finance and are thoroughly schooled in the art of keeping out of sight while Gentile dupes remain under the spotlight of the public eye, it is not known in what quantities they poured sums of money into Illuminati channels. But it is evident that from some secret source the movement had inexhaustible quantities to draw upon with which to carry out its brutal plot against Gentile civilization.

Karl Marx, the recognized father of modern Communism, edited his teachings out of the writings of Adam Weishaupt. The views expressed by both men are identical at many points. The first Communist Manifesto published by Marx in 1848 embodies both the principles and the spirit of the Illuminati.

Therefore, what we know as Communism today is the lineal descendant of the same anti-Christ conspiracy that brought about the French Revolution.

In his remarkable book *Are These Things So?*, Colonel E. N. Sanctuary discusses the three ring leaders who were largely responsible for revamping the Illuminati and preserving its root ideas. We read, "Marx, Lasalles, and Engels comprise the trio of Jews who, taking an altruistic theory, managed in a short time to turn it into a pronounced revolutionary doctrine, a doctrine that has left its scar on practically every civilized nation and which has so wounded some that they can not recover. Every cult and movement to a certain degree reflects the outstanding characteristics of the founders. Revolutionary socialism—now more commonly called communism—is no exception. The outstanding traits of these three men, which can be said to be outstanding traits of a large Jewish element, are found to predominate in the various groups that go to make up the present-day revolutionary movement. They are: Arrogance, intolerance, inflamed emotions, lack of ethical standards, and a desire for revenge, pronounced in Marx; immoral and unscrupulous acts, a demonic will, a disregard for the truth, the belief that to attain an end any means is justifiable, and a desire for ·revenge, pronounced in Lasalles; love of publicity, a desire to be thought 'progressive,' and a disposition to employ wealth attained through whatever means, to the advancement of subversive movements, pronounced in Engels.

"Another noticeable parallel between these three men and the vast majority of those now credited with being leaders in the world revolutionary movement— call it socialism or call it communism—is that none of them were 'wage-earners' or of the groups of citizens for whose welfare and uplift they insist they are working. Marx, to use good American slang, was a plain 'moocher.' Lasalles inherited a fortune and earned no money himself. Engels who was engaged with his father in the operation of cotton mills in which children were employed at scandalously low wages and for wickedly long hours, was a wealthy man.

"Karl Marx made popular, apparently, the well known Jewish system of adopting a name other than one's own. His name was not Marx but Mordecai. He came from a long line of rabbis although his father abandoned that profession and took up law. When Karl was about six years old the older Mordecai renounced the Jewish faith and embraced Christianity. Some of Marx's admirers attribute this action on the part of the elder Mordecai not to willingness but to pressure brought by governmental agencies. This is cited as one reason for Marx's presistent effort to destroy everything related to, or erected upon, the Christian faith. Regardless of the reason, in later years, as Marx associated more and more with the subversive elements, he took the position that the whole world was injured because of Christianity and believed—at least he urged—the revolutionary weapon as the one

and only means to correct the wrong. Of him Prof.
F. J. C. Hearnshaw writes: 'He was intolerant, bitter,
violent, venomous. . . . Nor was his ferocious intolerance a mere superficial defect of manner. It pene-
trated to the depths of his being and vitiated all his
thought. He was entirely lacking in the scientific
spirit, totally incapable of dispassionate argument.
His inflamed emotions determined his conclusion, and
his perverted intelligence put forth all its powers, with
a complete disregard of all moral scruples, to provide
an apparently rational foundation for them. . . Marx's
eminence is that of the agitator, not that of the think-
er. He did not make socialism scientific; he made it
predatory.' "

The parallelism between Weishaupt's teachings, the
French Revolution and the Russian Revolution is unmistakable.

It has been explained that the Illuminati was
Jewish. In like manner the Moscow dictatorship is
Jewish. When the bureaucracy was set up in Russia
eighteen years ago, it was headed by five hundred and
forty-five men, and of this number four hundred and
forty-seven were Jews, many of them having come
from the east side of New York. It has been established on the floor of the United States Congress that
a Jewish banking firm in Wall Street actually supplied
Lenin and Trotsky with the money to finance the Russian outbreak. Mrs. L. Fry points out in her book,
Waters Flowing Eastward that as far back as 1893-94
the Czar's government knew that Jacob Schiff, presi-
dent of the Kuhn, Loeb and Company bank in New
York, had been named chairman of the Committee on
the "Revolutionary Movement in Russia" by the B'nai
B'rith of the United States.

Another parallelism is the fact that Weishaupt
required the leaders of his Order to change their
names. In lodge parlance they also changed the names

of cities. Weishaupt took the title of Spartacus.

It was interesting to me to learn while in Germany that when the Reds first became active in that country a few years ago they did not call themselves Communists. They were known as Spartacusts, in memory of Weishaupt.

The Jewish leaders in Moscow likewise changed their names. Here are a few examples: Zederbaum became Lenin, Bronstein became Trotsky, Finklestein became Litvinoff, Sobelsohn became Rodak.

During the French Revolution, the Sabbath was destroyed. The same has been done in Russia.

Atheism was the national religion of the French Revolution. The same is true in Russia.

The Illuminati was correctly called a "subterranean fire". In view of the foregoing disclosures, who will say that the same flame is not burning today?

●

RUSSIA TODAY

WE have now learned that what history records as the French revolution was in reality the ripened fruit of an Illuminized and perverted Jewish Masonry. After years of preparation there was suddenly released, upon a dumfounded humanity, a torrent of misdirected energy which changed the face of all Europe.

Sparks from the conflagration blew in every direction and produced new flames in many parts of the world. Although a hundred and fifty years have elapsed since this holocaust took place, the forces thus set in motion have by no means spent themselves.

It is one thing to fight for an ideal and it is another thing to just fight for the sake of fighting. The Illuminati of the eighteenth century, like the Communism of today, developed a professional fierceness which feeds upon violence and human suffering. One overturn followed another as the appetites of the revolutionists became whetted for French blood.

The Moscow leaders have likewise continued their bestial crimes against the poor, helpless, exhausted Russian masses for eighteen years, in the name of perpetual revolution. They have reduced to a science, the idea that there should be no rest and peace for those who are governed. To them a revolution should be continuous, never allowed to come to an end. The formula is simple: if prosperity and contentment were to settle down upon the people, the revolutionists would be no longer needed; they would probably lose both their jobs and their heads.

Equally asinine are the frothings of street-corner Reds in the United States who demand the overthrow of the government under the guise of seeking to protect the liberties of the toilers. Any human being with an atom of common sense can see that the true purpose of the Communist organizers is simply to stir up strife and produce violence—because this is the way they make their living. They are paid by the ring of international despoilers to inflame the passions of those who listen to them. If it was a matter of personal conviction with them they would not be trying to tear down a system of democratic government under which the citizens have enjoyed more liberty, fraternity and equality than any other country in the history of the world .

Every American citizen can vote, exercise free speech, free press, accumulate property, expand his mind and heart without interference, and worship God according to the dictates of his own conscience. He has never had a king, tyrant or dictator to rule over him. He enjoys more personal liberty than any other type of citizen has ever enjoyed since governments began to exist on this earth. Yet the country is full of bass-voiced, leather-lunged, soap-box orators who are deliberately trying to create class hatred in the name of personal liberty and the mythological "forgotten man". As in the day of the Illuminati they are being directed from an occult, Jewish source far above them.

Any man who will live a good life, work hard, develop his mental faculties and take advantage of his opportunities for self advancement, can climb without restraint to the topmost rung of human achievement, under the American system of government. Note for instance, the thousands of men coming from the humblest and poorest walks of life, who have fitted themselves for positions of responsibility in the United States Senate, Congress and other positions of local and national government.

Instead of demanding the destruction of the American social order as it now exists, it would be more intelligent if agitators were to agitate for the purification of what we already have. Their inconsistency is at once evident. They are inconsistent because they are insincere. Yet this is the principle behind Illuminism, past and present. Illuminism has for its main purpose the intensifying of human restlessness as a means of tearing down everything that exists, so by long range advance preparation, the way may be paved for the powers behind the scenes to set up their final system of international government which proposes to reduce all Gentiles to the same state of slavery that exists in Soviet Russia at the present time.

Therefore, we discover that Communism is not a new thing. We have followed it back in a straight line to the year 1776. But even now, we have not traced it to its historic source. As an anti-Christ conspiracy, existing for the purpose of blotting out everything that bears the name of Christianity, its roots reach much deeper into the past than space has permitted us to show in this treatise.

No, Communism is not something that is designed to bless and enrich the poor and middle classes! It is not a movement to relieve human suffering. It did not originate with the down-trodden Russian masses. It did not break forth spontaneously eighteen years ago. It resulted from centuries of under-cover Jewish planning. Its final objective is to exhaust the human family in suffering and misery until the whole world can be brought under the heel of the merciless Jew-ocracy of Moscow which has been aptly called THE RED BEAST.

Books By Gerald B. Winrod

THE GREAT AMERICAN HOME

This is the complete text of a message delivered by Dr. Winrod containing a plea for national morality and a good home life, which he declares to be the bulwark of civilization. 24 pages _____20c

THE UNITED STATES AT THE CROSSROADS

Complete text of an address defending the Constitution of the United States and the great spiritual ideals upon which American civilization is built. A message which every Christian patriot should read. 24 pages _____20c

HEALING IN THE BIBLE

A remarkable compilation of Scripture, accompanied by terse comments, showing the large place which the Ministry of Healing occupies in the Word of God. 20 pages. _____15c

GOD REVEALED

God is not discovered. He is revealed. Four revelations of Him are discussed. 20 pages _____10c

CHRIST WITHIN

The reader's heart will be strongly warmed as he reads the chapter on "Christ Within". Three other chapters also. 138 pages _____$1.25

SCIENCE, CHRIST AND THE BIBLE

This volume contains the complete text of ten scholarly addresses delivered by the Author before large audiences in the United States, Canada and the West Indies. 160 pages. $1.25

THE KEYSTONE OF CHRISTIANITY

Powerful, thought-provoking addresses on vital themes: spiritual, scientific, logical and illuminating. 138 pages. _____$1.25

BIBLE STORIES OF THE WISE FAMILY

By Mrs. Gerald B. Winrod. This booklet is a charming Bible Story Book for children under fifteen years of age. 52 pages. _____25c

THE TABERNACLE, TEMPLE AND THRONE

By Mrs. Gerald B. Winrod. A book dealing for most part with the subject of the Tabernacle in the Wilderness, explaining the typology of this remarkable structure for which God gave Moses the pattern. 80 pages. _____25c

REDEEMING THE YEARS THE LOCUST HATH EATEN

By Rev. J. W. Winrod. A condensed Autobiography. Tells how the Author grew up with the boy who later became General Pershing. Mr. Winrod was the proprietor of the first saloon Carry Nation ever smashed. Today he is a Minister of the Gospel. 36 pages. _____25c

TRACTS BY DR. WINROD

"Is America Seeing Red?" "Liberalism, Socialism and Communism", "Blind Leaders of the Blind", "Modernism and the Crisis of the Church", "Where are the Mystics?" "Should We Eat Pork?" "Eagle-Saints", "The Tragic Experience of Mary Lou", "The Blunder of Atheism", "Snakes in an Atheist's Grave", "Come, Tarry, Go", "The Story of Puerto Rico", "Paul of the Kru Tribe", "The Black Prophet", "The HOW of the Translation of the Church", "Wars and Rumors of Wars", "Violence Filled the Earth", "World Problems", "Angels and Demons", "Belshazzar's Feast", "Is the U. S. on the Verge of War?" "The Holy Spirit", "Jewish-Communism, the International Foe of Christianity", "Human Vipers", "The Prophetic Message of the Beatitudes" and "A Methodist Parable".

All Tracts are the same price: three for 5 cents; one dozen 15 cents; one hundred $1.00.

DEFENDER PUBLISHERS, Wichita, Kansas

www.ingramcontent.com/pod-product-compliance
Lightning Source LLC
Chambersburg PA
CBHW071233290326
41931CB00037B/2930